DIARY OF A ZOMBIE KID

THE JOURNAL OF BILL STOKES

by Fred Perry & David Hutchison

Antarctic Press
San Antonio, Texas

DIARY OF A ZOMBIE KID ™

Writer - Fred Perry
Artists - David Hutchison & Fred Perry
Inspiration & Concept - Brian Denham & Joe Dunn
Editors - Robby Bevard & Doug Dlin
Graphic Designer - GURU-eFX
Cover Design - GURU-eFX
Layout - Doug Dlin

Editor in Chief - Jochen Weltjens
President of Sales and Marketing - Lee Duhig
Art Direction - GURU-eFX
VP of Production - Wes Hartman
Publishing Manager - Robby Bevard
Publisher - Joe Dunn
Founder - Ben Dunn

Come visit us online at www.antarctic-press.com

Diary of a Zombie Kid by Fred Perry
and David Hutchison

Antarctic Press
7272 Wurzbach Suite 204 San Antonio, TX 78240

ISBN: 978-0-9831823-3-7
Printed and bound Canada.

Sunday
Partly Cloudy.
Oatmeal.
Call of Fragenator-4:
51 kills,
x3 Blast Streaks.

ICK

This is only a replacement diary. I lost my first one
in the fire...the fire my dad got arrested for setting.
Shoot, I should probably talk about that first so
this temporary diary has some kind of link to the
past. I'll need that in case the insurance agent or
fire department or whoever is going through our old,
burnt-out house can't find my first diary.

I'm Bill. Bill Stokes. I started my first diary to keep
track of my video game high scores. My friends back

at the old cul-de-sac all kept records of high scores in little notebooks for bragging rights. I wanted a bragging book too, and there was this diary in the bargain bin at the S-Mart, so I used that.

Larry from across the street thought he was slick for using his cell phone to keep track, until he accidentally dropped that phone into his sheepdog's food dish! Poor Wolfenstein was rickrolling the "Never Gonna Give You Up" ringtone from his stomach every time someone dialed Larry's number!

Never gonna let you down...

The whole thing must have been pretty traumatic to the phone, because by the time the vet got it back to Larry, its memory was a total blank!

I started writing more and more stuff in my good old, dependable score book: what I had for breakfast, what the weather outside was...any details that might have affected my high score. Eventually, I started writing down what I did and what I was feeling. So my score book became a sort of a diary. This all has a purpose, though.

Someday, when I become a pro gamer—and the pro gamer career path IS coming...SOON—I'll be able to feed all this data into a computer, and it'll give me the stats back for the perfect conditions for my perfect pre-game set up.

Having info going back all the way to today, the first day of middle school, is going to be my championship edge!

Being a pro gamer is like being a rock star or a movie star. I saw this one pro in an internet video last year. He had crowds of fans calling his name and got millions of hits on his website! He tours the tournament circuit, winning thousands and thousands of dollars... and he's an awful player!

Soon, pro gamers are going to be just as big as pro athletes...and I've got the skill and the talent to be the greatest one of all. The only thing that can possibly stand in my way is middle school!

I'd still like to have all the data I put down in my first diary, though. I'm glad Dad got arrested for what he did. I hope he stays in jail! I guess I should write that here so that future computer-statistic analyzer can factor this in.

Dad lost his job at the investment banker firm a month ago, and has been out of work ever since. They said he was cheating or something. He just stayed at home, got drunk and picked on Mom and me.

Dad threw a shoe at me for spilling milk on the carpet once, and he yelled at Mom a lot. It was hard to concentrate on my games all last month because of that. Those bad scores are noted in my first diary.

The day before the fire, I think Dad bought some insurance. They arrested him for arson and trying to run a scam. Good. I can't stand cheaters! I can't stand bullies! When things weren't going his way, Dad became both.

For a while, Mom didn't know what to do. She never had a job before, but she seems to be doing okay now. She got a job and this apartment, so things are getting back to normal again (especially because I managed to save my game system and my games from the fire). I guess I pack pretty fast when I want to.

Mom's new "job," as she calls it, is as a medicine test volunteer for various companies. She earns quite a lot for such little effort. I'm hoping this is temporary and she finds a real job soon, mainly because there are days when she comes home really woozy.

Other than that, we're doing okay now.

Monday

Partly Cloudy.

Frosted Sugar Tufts.

Call of Fragenator-4: 30 kills, x2 Blast Streaks.

Super Street Masher 4 (Arcade Edition): 35
Consecutive Online Wins. 6 Perfects.

Today was the first day of middle school in this new
district. The trauma definitely messed up my after-
school gaming practice performance!

I wasn't expecting any of the crud that fell on me
today, even after all the research I did on middle
school. Yes, I researched middle school. If there's
a new game, I'm going to learn everything about it

before I even touch the controller. Experimenting without prep work is for newbies and wastes time. This goes for IRL* "games" too—"games" like middle school. Research that stuff before you jump in.

The thing is, all the research I gathered on middle school didn't help one bit. I wore the most average-looking clothes and tried my best to blend.

I didn't want to mess with any of these guys, I just wanted to be invisible and not have to deal with anyone. Middle school doesn't count—nothing counts in life until you get into the 9th grade! I've got no friends and no rich parents. My best move, from now until graduation, is to lay low.

*IRL — In Real Life, for future historians.

Unfortunately, I was noticed by this weirdo, Janine. Janine, who seems to eat, breathe and sleep "Hiya Kitty". What does she want with me?

Luckily, my old cul-de-sac buddy Larry's in this school. He's still got his notebook too. Larry's no competition, but at least he's there to keep the bar from getting too low for me. He knows what's going to happen on the pro gamer scene: It's gonna be big, and he'll be in there. Not a star like me, but he'll have some fans. I can hang with Larry, especially if it means I can talk to him and pretend not to hear Janine calling during lunch.

Janine wouldn't give it a rest, though. She sat right with us at lunch and just started saying a lot of nothing about nothing. She wouldn't take a hint, and she drew too much attention. She asked if I'm antisocial or something. NO!

WHAT CHIMPS MIGHT LOOK LIKE

If you're stuck in a chimp pen at the zoo, you keep quiet and don't attract the attention of dumb chimps, or you'll get poop flung at you! Common sense!

She didn't know better, and rambled against me, "But a zoo has more than just monkeys! Don't forget the zebras and the koalas and the panda bears! You'd make a nice, clever little turtle, and I'm probably a kitty. Oh, maybe a meerkat!"

She just went on and on, like she didn't even hear what I was trying to say!

Sure enough, some "chimps" were drawn to Janine's loud colors and "Bitts-Maru" hair clips to check out the freak. One was an idiot named Steve from eighth grade—big guy with bad breath, a long basketball jersey with pants that he wore around his knees, and stubble on his eighth-grade unshaven chin. He snatched up our snack cakes—an obvious test to check if we were complainers, squealers, toadies or wimps.

Putting up a finger, I spat out, "Uh...I sneezed on that." Then I sniffed a loud, phlegm-filled sniff. He put my cake down and looked at me. Shoot! I'd made a mistake! I could see it in the small, pimply face of his big, fat head, him registering a title under my silhouette and profile: "Wiseguy."

Hatebook

STATUS UPDATE:

WISEGUY

He let the incident go and continued on his merry rounds of bullying less intelligent victims. I decided I would have to disguise my profile tomorrow, maybe fade out of memory and avoid any future crud from that chimp. HOWEVER...

Janine turned around and said, in her outdoor voice, "Ha ha! That was awesome!"

Steve stopped. He slowly wheeled around and strolled back to the table. He took my snack cake and pointed a meaty finger at my nose for a few seconds before continuing on his way.

Perfect. Now I have a bully.

For the rest of lunch, I had to listen to Janine make zoo animals out of everyone in the cafeteria. She wouldn't shut up or stop saying I was a "turtle." Hmm. Maybe I now have two bullies.

by Janine

When I came home, I breezed through the easy-mode homework assignments, making sure to leave a few glaring mistakes in order to guarantee a "B minus" to "C plus". I've read about the hazards of getting shunted into advance placement classes. I'd rather not risk my future as the worlds greatest pro gamer.

Mom got home from her new "job" and fixed dinner. She was really woozy again, though; her job seems to take a lot out of her.

Dinner tasted funny. Not bad funny, but weird funny. I didn't finish mine. I ate slowly and waited for Mom to finish before I put mine in the dumpster in back of our apartment. Advantages of the ground floor. Good night.

Weird dream. I dreamed my stomach was being eaten by ants! I woke up, and my stomach felt a little queasy, but it wasn't hurting. Soon after that, I heard something weird going on out back near the dumpster, like there was some nasty cat fight. Man, it was loud! Somebody's cat was getting beaten up!

I went to the kitchen to see what was going on because those cats were getting scary-loud! It was so noisy, someone called the cops and the animal shelter! I saw it happening from the kitchen window. This really mean, scary-looking cat was all scarred and stuff!

It tore the loop when the guy from the animal shelter tried to put a noose around its neck to capture it. Then it jumped and scratched the heck out of that policeman's face! It was a really, REALLY harsh scratch, too!

I noticed two other cats around the dumpster as well. They were all freaky-looking too, and moving weird.

And MEAN! One of the policemen shot the BOSS cat when it tried to lunge again, but the cat got back up! It's like it was a zombie or something! The cop that got his face scratched shot three times, and it looked like those three cats were all hit in the head! That ended it! Man, that was scary!

I called Mom, but she just moaned and stayed in bed. This night was weird. Really, really weird!

I hope it doesn't affect my scores.

Tuesday

Rainy.

½ bowl of Frosted Sugar Tufts.

Call of Fragenator-4: 45 kills, x6 Blast Streaks.

Super Street Masher 4 (Arcade Edition): 38 Consecutive Online Wins. 10 Perfects.

Felt really strange today, all through the morning and all the way up until lunch. You know how your arm feels when you sleep on it? All rubbery with no feeling in it, but you can move it? That's how my whole body felt! Numb and everything. I couldn't even feel if the water was hot or cold when I took a shower. Mom was shuffling her feet all morning too.

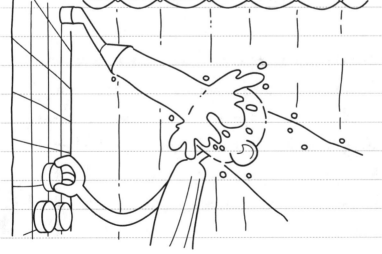

She looked real stuffed-up and droopy-faced. She also had this creepy, blank stare in her eyes. If she's got a cold, I hope I don't get it.

During lunch, Larry was talking about the Game-Stuff shop at the mall and the *Call of Fragenator* tournament they were having. This was good news, because I knew that prize money would be mine if I could scrape together the $30 entrance fee. Larry said he was going to mow some lawns to get the money.

Pfft. Counter-productive. The best way is to shark some college guys for money-matches in *Super Street Masher 4* at the Putt-and-Golf! You can rake in an easy $100 in just ten minutes if you scout your victims properly.

Something was distracting me about Larry as we were making plans for the tournament. He smelled like he was dunked in chocolate syrup! The whole time Larry was talking, he smelled like a candy bar. He smelled better than my lunch tray—which, by the way, tasted a little like the lunch lady had spilled some mud in the mashed potatoes.

We finished eating quickly enough to avoid Janine, who was just getting out of the lunch line by the time we were standing up. I wore a poker face to hide any amusement at seeing her look of disappointment from being left all alone at the table.

Poker Face

I practice my poker face every chance I get! It once saved my life after I accidentally sharked a sore loser in his late twenties at the arcade last summer.

Steve was still stuck in the lunch line too when we left. Speed wins again.

The weird, numb feeling stuck with me all through the day. I didn't even feel it when Steve threw that eraser at my head in the hall after school let out.

After I finished making sure my homework was C-minus worthy, I got to game practice. I didn't think the numb feeling would let me do too well, but wow! It's like there was no delay between my brain and the controller.

I couldn't do my combos, but I could react instantly to anything! Then I'd go sluggish after that first "surprise attack". Anyway, I won more just by remaining perfectly still, then leaping on any opening instantly with the correct move. Maybe I found my winning technique?

Mom didn't make dinner. She just shuffled around the house aimlessly, like she was looking for something but didn't know what she wanted. That's okay, because I wasn't really hungry. Except for maybe a weird craving for chocolate syrup?

<u>Wednesday</u>

Overcast.

Skipped Breakfast.

Atomic VS Discom 3: 12 Consecutive Online Wins. 6 Perfects.

I almost woke up late for school today. The alarm clock was going off when I rose, but it's like I didn't hear it when I was asleep.

It must have been that really weird dream I had! The class was full of chocolate syrup-covered animal crackers—horses, bears, monkeys, and one kitty!

It seemed like they were all throwing erasers at me and laughing. I tried to tell them to stop. The dream ended when the big, ugly gorilla cookie punched me right in the face, but his cookie fist crumbled! Yet, somehow, I knew it would do that.

What woke me up was the faint smell of burning cheese. You know that nasty-smelling cheese that tastes like someone's gym sock? Imagine that burning and stinking up the whole house.

I got cleaned up, dressed, and then came down to see Mom slumping around the kitchen. My burnt-up cheese sandwich was on the table with some juice to wash it down. I could see there was supposed to be some waffles and strawberry jam, but Mom must not have gotten her coordination back, because there was strawberry jam all over the table and on the floor.

While she was bending over to wipe up the mess, and taking her sweet, sluggish, time doing it, she stepped in some jam and slipped, and wow! Mom hit the floor hard! NOSE-DIVED it! Cracked some kitchen floor tiles, too! WHABAM!

THUD

I tried to hurry to her, but I guess I wasn't all the way awake yet, because my feet felt like I had iron shoes on. That's okay, because Mom was fine! She got up like it'd never happened! But it did happen. She still had some flecks of kitchen tile fragments stuck to her face as she slumped away. I think she got sick at work, 'cause she's really been out of it the past few days. I hope I haven't caught what she has...

So there I was, alone in the kitchen with the stinky cheese sandwich! All burnt up, nasty and black-looking. The toast crust all charcoaly. But I was hungry! I was so hungry that I not only failed to hurl when I lifted that stink sandwich to my mouth, I could feel some drool escape as I ALMOST bit down.

I stopped. I thought about how even the smallest bite
would make my breath extra stinky alllll day long. So,
I put the sandwich into the trash and went for my
Frosted Sugar Tufts. They were kind of stale and
tasted a little like sand instead of sugar. I suppose I
got a bad batch from a bad box. Anyway, I was running
late, and the school bus wasn't going to wait. I had to
leave the cereal and milk out for Mom to put up.

I was still feeling real numb when I got into class.
The air conditioner was on the blink, and kids were
complaining it was getting too muggy, but I didn't
mind so much. The only thing that got to me was this
faint chocolate syrup smell, but no one else seemed to
notice. Maybe there's something wrong with my nose.

For science lab, we were supposed to be dissecting great big worms, but some wise guy gave me a realistic looking gummy-worm instead. I knew it for what it was right away. It didn't smell like formaldehyde or alcohol or any kind of preservative like it was supposed to. Plus, you can just tell when something is made of candy. Good fake, though.

I bet it was Larry trying to get one over on me. Back when we were at the cul-de-sac, I gave him some puke-flavored beans from this bag of "any-flavor" novelty jelly beans. He's been trying to get me back ever since. I'd guessed his plan this time.

Larry was going to come up as my lab partner, talk about dissecting the worm for a while, pretend to go along with the lab, then he'd try to gross me out by eating the gummy worm right in front of me. Nice try, but I'm win-tier!

As soon as he came up with our lab paper printouts, I made a nice, big show of eating the gummy worm right in his face. I must have taken him by surprise, because his eyes bugged out and his face turned green! The gummy worm was peach—flavored. My favorite! He hurled.

I laughed and told him I'd found his gummy worm. Maybe he was grossed out in thinking I'd really eaten a worm! He wouldn't fess up that he'd switched worms, so while he took a trip to the nurse's office, I got an "F" in the lab and a talk from the vice principal.

Larry swore up and down that he didn't pull a switch. Maybe he didn't want me to find the novelty brand label. They make convincing, tasty worms and probably have other tricks he's going to try to punk me with.

Strangely enough, I didn't feel like eating lunch at all today. It smelled like ash, anyway. I need to talk to somebody about that lunch lady. Someone needs to call the health department on her.

Janine avoided me today, probably because of the worm incident. Good! The fewer distractions, the better. Although she was talking to Larry some...and smiling. I need to ask Larry what they were talking about sometime.

When I got home, I didn't even bother with homework. I'll get a zero, but I can make it up over the course of the next six assignments with a string of B-minuses. That way, I keep my nice, efficient C-minus average. My win record on the new crossover fighting game was pretty impressive. That, or no one else knows how to play yet.

I just remained perfectly still and reacted to any opening that appeared. I was winning so easily that I stopped practicing early. I can't improve if I'm not challenged. Maybe I should give the newbies more time to get better before I come back to that game.

Thursday
Partly Cloudy
Soggy, Sour, Stale Frosted Sugar Tufts.
Atomic VS Discom 3: 12 Consecutive Online Wins.
11 Perfects.

Mom might still be sick. She's been seriously out of
it ever since she came back from her medicine testing
"job" on Monday. But today it's like she's on autopilot
or something.

This morning, when I got to the kitchen, there was
milk all over the table and eggs burning in the skillet
on the stove. Mom was still pouring cereal from the
carton into the bowl, spilling it out of the bowl and
all over the table! It's like she can't even use her
arms right anymore. Breakfast was a mess!

I must have been really hungry or something, though, because those burnt-up eggs and stuff were smelling good just about the time they were getting all black and greasy! I thought about trying them, but Mom was snarling and wolfing them down out of the skillet before I knew it.

I backed off before I lost a finger or an arm! Man, I didn't even want to get near Mom while she was tearing into that burnt-up egg stuff.

I went for my cereal bowl. The milk was a little sour...okay, maybe a lot sour! And the cereal was moldy, but I didn't notice until I was halfway through the bowl! You know what's weird? I didn't instinctively gag on what was inside. It tasted great that way. That cereal was the first thing that tasted good to me in three days! Then again, nothing's tasted right since Mom made dinner on Monday night.

I'm putting down what happened at breakfast, in full detail, for a reason: The rest of the day sort of combo'd off that, and not in a good way!

We had a geometry pop quiz in math today. Easy mode. I had to concentrate in order to keep my score nice and average, so I can focus on practicing for my future career as a world champion pro gamer!

During that pop quiz, the breakfast I thought I had totally defeated began its counter-attack! It was the loudest, densest, foulest, most evil fart that had ever, EVER been brought to this planet Earth!

The windows rattled, the floor shook, pencils vibrated from the tops of desks, and it took us all, including me, by complete surprise! When it was over, there was nothing but silence! No one knew where to look! The

sound had bounced around the room so that it was coming from everywhere at once!

Then the aroma came, like sour milk and roadkill! All at once, everyone in the class held their noses and "Ewww"ed. The kid behind me passed out! At that point, I started to panic. Everyone would be able to figure out the source of the blast by its area of strongest effect!

Playing games in tournaments makes you think on your feet, though. I pointed at Harold, the fat kid sitting in front of me, and faked passing out! That did it! Everyone else followed my example and pointed too! The teacher even bought it!

Everyone complained and yelled and fussed at Harold while we evacuated the class! Harold is now known forevermore as "Death-Butt"!

Sorry, Harold. I just don't need that kind of attention. School's going to be tough enough now that I'm a zombie.

Yeah, that's what's going on. I'm a zombie.

I prefer rotten stuff to eat. I have the guts of a dead horse. My reaction time is through the roof, while I'm a turtle after the lightning-quick jump from the starting line. That death gas was a zombie's fart!

The virus Mom brought back on Monday changed me somehow. I think Mom's a zombie too, but she's way more out of it than I am.

The thing is, what am I going to do now? How am I going to make my dream of being the world's greatest pro gamer become a reality if I'm a zombie?

I scored even more perfects today in AvD3. Everybody online complains about my turtle "zombie" style. But a win is a win, even if I'm just doing super-fast reaction-type play.

Hmmm. Maybe this can work out somehow after all!

Friday
Sunny
(You probably don't want to know what I had for breakfast today.)
Atomic Vs. Discom 3: 20 Consecutive Wins. 16 Perfects.

Let's skip the breakfast description today, or maybe just breeze over it. Even I couldn't believe what Mom made for me today—or that I thought it tasted pretty good! I'll say this, though: I only had a little before I was full.

Remember that song everyone sings to gross themselves out? "Great, green gobs of greasy, grimy gopher guts"? If you'd looked into the big pot of stuff that Mom was stirring, you'd think that song was the alternate recipe list! All different ingredients except the "little, dirty birdie feet". I could see them bobbing as the whole mess came to a boil. It smelled awesome. Even as a zombie, Mom has a talent for making stuff taste good!

I shuffled over to the table and sat down, and Mom gave me a half-crooked zombie smile. I guess she knew, and it seemed things would be sort of normal around the house. For a second, I thought that maybe I wouldn't have to go to school anymore, now that we were zombies. If ever there was a "stay at home for health" excuse, catching a zombie virus would be at the top! But nooooo.

After breakfast, Mom got my book bag and my coat, then grunted a zombie-mom grunt as she shoved them at me. She still expected me to go to school! I tried to explain. I tried to tell her that school is for kids who aren't zombified, but she wouldn't listen!

She pushed me out of the house into that burning morning sunlight. Good thing there were plenty of shade trees to hide under. But, great...from that moment on, I knew I would have to deal with school, the threat of a zombie sunburn, a zombie mom who won't listen, bullies...and then I smelled it. My breath. My death breath!

My breath STUNK from that zombie breakfast! I let an "Uh-oh!" slip from my lips. Almost immediately, some birds up in the tree shrieked and flapped wildly. It was like someone had hit two flies with a can of bug spray! The birds fell dead at my feet, and some wilted leaves slowly fluttered down afterward.

ZOMBIE DEATH BREATH! I knew right then that I would have to keep my lips shut for the entire day!

I focused on making a game plan for that day. The best I could come up with was to get Larry's attention immediately and get him to guess that I had a sore tooth!

Larry has always been quick to pick up on hints, and I knew he was the perfect guy to act as an interpreter for anyone not fast enough to get a clue. Everything would have worked out for the whole day if it wasn't for Mrs. McGillicuddy, our school nurse.

Mrs. McGillicuddy is the total combination of everybody's weird aunt rolled up into one great, big package. She pinches cheeks, kisses "booboos" right before putting on the antiseptic, gives a piece of candy to anyone who comes to the nurse's office, and treats us all like we're in preschool. Plus, she's super-sized! So I guess everybody would look like a baby to her, even the other teachers!

Mrs. McGillicuddy wanted to see my tooth before I went home today. She said she was earning her nursing license at a dental school and wanted to make sure nothing was infected. I wrote her a note saying it wasn't hurting anymore, but she kept trying to get me to open my mouth. I wrote another note saying Mom was going to take me to the dentist after school. That should have been the end of that.

No, not for Mrs. McGillicuddy. She insisted and started wagging her finger in my face. I knew the stink had been sitting in my mouth all day, just waiting for a victim. Mrs. McGillicuddy was playing with forces she couldn't possibly comprehend.

Then it happened. She lost her patience, grabbed my face, pulled down my jaw and stuck her nose right into my open mouth. I swear, I could actually see her curly brown hair crinkle into craggy, grey knots!

I noticed her eyes, already lifeless, rolling back into her head as she fell backward onto the sick bed. Her fingers lost all strength and dropped away as the sick bed buckled under her mass!

I hoped I hadn't killed her. I didn't check to see. I just got out of there. I was really scared she might be dead. I made it to my bus just in time to see her being pulled from the school and out into the fresh air. She had this dazed, confused look on her face. Whew. I have to be more careful.

I cleaned out my mouth with a ton of mouthwash to kill all the germs. That did the trick. I'll have to be extra-careful with my new zombie biology.

Saturday

Sunny

Leftover zombie stew and a lot of mouthwash.
Call of Fragenator Tournament: Won in Winners
Bracket. 12 Blast Streaks.

I didn't sleep in today. The *Call of Fragenator*
tournament started today down at the Game-Stuff,
so I woke up early to get as much warm-up practice
in as I could. I knew the tournament was in the bag,
though. No one could beat my zombie-style game play.

All I had to do in game was hang out in dark alleys and
places with lots of blind corners. My zombie reactions
could handle the rest.

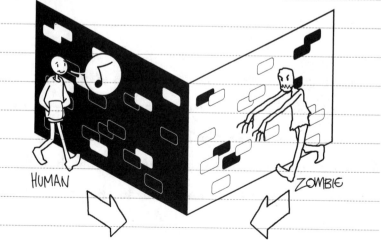

HUMAN   ZOMBIE

Anyone rounding a corner or entering the alley would get jumped on and destroyed before they could do anything!

The tournament was a non-issue; the trick was getting that registration fee! That, and getting Mom to drive me to the mall today. The question was if Mom could still drive her car. The answer was yes...a very scary yes!

If you're ever in a car and a zombie is at the wheel, and you're not a zombie yourself, wear a helmet! Well, obviously, but not for the exact reasons you think. Mom pushed down on the gas reeeally slowly...but she let up on the gas really slowly too, so that brake pedal was getting the workout of its lifetime warranty!

Creepy-slow accelerations, then breakneck sudden stops and turns all the way! We didn't hit anybody, but we probably scared the bees out of everyone Mom cut in front of with her zombie driving!

We parked up in front of the big bookstore with the coffee shop in it, like we do every Saturday. I guess, zombie or not, Mom's getting her coffee and CosMom. The thing is, she didn't even have to say what kind of coffee she wanted. The coffee shop guys saw her coming and started making "the usual"!

This made me a little hopeful for the future. Mom's a real zombie, and no one notices. Maybe being a zombie isn't that big a deal. Or maybe it takes someone getting eaten before everyone notices there's a zombie in the room.

Hmmm...you know, I never really thought of eating people before. I wonder what they taste like?

As usual, Mom sat in that booth in the corner, and I waited for her to give me my allowance. I thought it took forever for her to give me my cash before. This time, I had to wait a half-hour before she finished that first sip of coffee! Point-five hours! It took five whole minutes for her to unzip her purse! UGH!

Just thinking about it makes me want to scratch my nails on a chalkboard. I don't know where I got the extra patience, but I managed to wait. Mom gave me my twenty. Finally!!

While Mom continued taking her caffeine drink as slowly as inhumanly possible, I switched to my fighting game scamming mode!

Step 1: Go into the bookstore's magazine aisle and buy the most newbie-ish-looking game magazine I could find with hints on the latest fighting game! So I had to spend about five bucks. Investment.

Step 2: Head to the Putt-and-Golf just across the street from the mall and scout the victims! Three guys. One dude dragged his bored girlfriend along. They were playing Super Street Masher 4 Arcade

Edition...badly. It's funny how everyone wants to be like those pro-gaming superstars from Japan we all see on YouVid, but no one understands what makes them superstars: practice AND talent AND smarts. These guys didn't seem to have any of that going for them.

Step 3: Wait for my turn to play the winner, making sure all victims see me as I pretend to read the newbie-ish game magazine for hints on how to win!

Step 4: Pretend I don't know what I'm doing when I first play. Make sure I win by a really narrow margin and that the winning move looks like a complete accident!

Step 5: Be a sore newbie winner! This was the hard part. I had to be convincing. I had to be really arrogant and cocky, so I made them think that I was a newbie who got lucky and needed to be taken down a peg.

THAT'S when I asked for the money match! My ten dollars versus their ten dollars! After that, I just

made it look like it was luck or that the game was favoring my approach. That's the key! It's critical that I make it seem like it was the game's fault or that they lost because of bad luck, not because of me!

I earned sixty bucks from those high school kids, and they never even suspected my skill. That is, until one of them saw me later that day while I was racking up the frags in the Game-Stuff tournament. Heh heh. That's 130 bucks, plus the satisfaction of seeing an older high school kid realize just how win-tier I am! Today was a sweet day!

Sunday

Skipped breakfast

No gameplay: "Cool down and reflect" time after
tourney!

I wasn't hungry at all this morning. Not for any
leftover zombie stew, at least. That was lucky,
because there wasn't any to eat, regardless. By the
time I came down to see what Mom was doing in the
kitchen, she was scraping the bottom of the stew pot
with what I hoped was a soup bone.

The pot was empty down to the last drop. Mom did save a little bit for me, but as soon as she saw I wasn't interested, it was gone! I'll have to remember that: zombie-moms only give you one chance to eat your breakfast. ONE.

I spent the rest of the day taking care of my weekend homework and checking the internet for replay videos from professional tournaments. It seems someone filmed the tournament I was in just yesterday. The commentators started calling me "Kid Dracula" because of my "lurking in the shadows"-style gameplay. Hmm. It didn't take them long to figure out what I was doing to win. I'll need to change up my combat style so no one can develop counter-strategies.

It did kind of make me laugh out loud when the commentators started yelping in surprise from my sudden attacks on my victims. It was like they were watching some monster movie and talking about it to the tournament's online video-stream viewers.

"Kid Dracula." I like the sound of that. I think I'll change my online gamer tag to that tomorrow.

I also noticed something odd going on in the pro gamer online community. I saw this new fighting game, something called Super Smasher Sisters, picking up a lot of steam. It might be the next big thing.

The game's got a lot of cutesy characters in it, but the gameplay is really smooth and innovative. Just from the videos, I could see there was a lot of strategy involved in winning, but the controls seemed easy enough for anyone to pick up. Even better, the set-up made it difficult for people to abuse low-risk moves easily. It's a well thought-out system that takes a minute to learn and forever to master. That's the kind of game that'll get a lot of fans in a hurry, the kind that's gonna be big on the scene, and soon! Lots of tournaments, lots of cash prizes.

Right then and there, I knew I'd have to get in on this one from the ground floor. Only one thing kind of made me nervous: this player whose online name was "SanReaper"!

Whoever this dude was, he was a beast! Awesome strategy! Awesome setups! And it really looked like he was having fun with the game.

Hmm. I need to get this game ASAP! I need to get in on this!

<u>Monday</u>

Squirrel surprise

Super Smasher Sisters (at Larry's): 25 consecutive wins against Larry. 13 perfects.

When I came down to the kitchen this morning, Mom already had a ton of junk boiling in the stew pot...the unwashed stew pot. On the counter, there were pieces of diced earthworm. I'm still amazed my gag-o-meter hasn't gone off! I can't believe I snuck a piece and slurped my fingers after that!

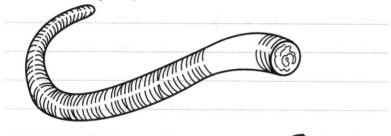

They look gross to my brain, but my stomach, tongue, and nose tell me they're like sugary slices of orange. While I'm seeing charred toad guts on the plate and going onto my spoon, I'm smelling and tasting creamy, extra-cheesy macaroni.

I sat down at the kitchen table. The kitchen was kind of messy, but I could see where Mom was keeping things looking semi-normal. I guess she's still trying to continue a normal life.

From the kitchen window, I spotted her in the back yard, standing right next to the pear tree. Her arms were out like branches. She was perfectly still. Incredibly still. I didn't think she was breathing! I thought she was dead...extra-dead!

Before I could run outside to check, a squirrel ran up Mom's side with a mouth full of nuts. As soon as that sucker got near mom's face—BAM!—Mom caught it in her teeth!

The squirrel became her victim. I mean, wow! Her head was as fast as a cobra's! I had no idea zombies could do that too.

She came into the kitchen after that. Put the sucker in the pot—bones, fur and all—then started stirring. And that was breakfast: squirrel surprise. Maybe I should call it "surprised squirrel"?

After breakfast, I immediately killed all the odor in my mouth. I can't EVER forget to do that!

I was leaving for school, and I got to the door. I checked the mirror to make sure nothing was wrong, and then I saw it: this huge pimple on my chin!

No, it was too big to be a pimple. This was a cyst! What the heck was goin' on with my anatomy? I studied it closer in the mirror, and I could almost see the black liquid pooling underneath my skin. No way I was heading to school with that on my face. I had to try to pop it. This is when I discovered how tough a zombie zit can be!

I tried just squeezing it. Nope. It just filled with more black fluid and got bigger and nastier. I got my sharpest pencil and tried spearing it open. Nope. The zit broke my pencil! BROKE IT! I looked again, and the zit had grown to the the size of a peanut candy!

It just hung there and jiggled whenever I so much as
moved my head or opened my mouth to speak! If ever
there was an excuse to stay home sick, I now had it.
No parent in their right mind would send their child
to school with this nasty, pulsating, black-green pimple
on their chin. (It turned a little green after it
kicked my pencil's butt.)

Not MY Mom. She was right there before I could
turn around from the door, blank-staring, but looking
right at me. She went, "HNNNnnnnnn!" which meant,
"Bill, you better get your butt to school!"

I pointed at the pimple. She acted like she didn't even see it, but I knew she did, and she didn't give a hoot! Even as a zombie, Mom's autopilot works! There could be a flood, a meteor from space could wipe out half of Mankind, and zombies could walk the Earth. (Whoa, hey! How about that?) Mom would still insist on me going to school!

Anyway, back to the ZIT! My only chance was to tuck my chin into my chest and pull my shirt up over my mouth. I thought I would look like some kind of bandito and maybe even make a slightly cool fashion statement. Something the other kids might look at for a second and go, "Hey, that's kinda different."

At the same time, it wouldn't be so strange that I'd attract unwanted attention. I got my hopes up and didn't check the mirror to make sure I wasn't making things worse. WHY didn't I just look in the mirror?

I could tell just from the way everyone stared at me on the bus and from everyone snirking and giggling in homeroom that I had made a gigantic mistake! I was trapped—trapped in my decision to do this. I could feel that ZIT against my chest, just pulsing and growing! It was the size of a dime now, and if I pulled my chin out at that point, with everyone paying so much attention to me, I'd strike the entire class unconscious with laughter!

Then, as I knew she would, zoo-headed Janine just had to go and open her big mouth and say, "See! I knew you were a clever little turtle-boy!"

It took five minutes for the teacher to settle the class down from laughing. Strangely enough, Janine was the only one who didn't get her own joke! She looked around confused! I bet she thought she was giving me a compliment! What an airhead!

I would have spent the whole day like that if it weren't for the ZIT's auto-destruct sequence. It was just about lunchtime, and by now my black-and-green chin-cyst was the size of a quarter, when something popped under my shirt! It was like a water balloon filled with ink!

I ducked into the bathroom to check myself out in the stall and, sure enough, the cyst had broken under its own massive weight. It's a good thing my shirt was black, because if I'd worn anything else, it would have looked like six pens had exploded on my chest.

My chin healed while I watched in the mirror. I mean fast—crazy fast! The scab fell off before I could scratch it! Whatever this zombie virus did to me, my immune system seemed to like it. Come to think of it, I haven't had a stuffy nose since last week! Hmmm.

I got some paper towels to wipe the black fluid off my chest and shirt and checked to make sure it didn't stink. I guess that was lucky. Not everything inside a zombie stinks to high heaven when it spills out.

Before leaving the bathroom, I checked to see what everyone was laughing at. I tucked my chin down and pulled my shirt over my mouth again. I looked just like a turtle with his head half out of his shell! Why didn't I check this out before I left the house this morning? WHY?

WHY
DIDN'T I
CHECK?

I pretended to eat that mud-tasting food they serve
at the cafeteria, just to keep up appearances. Larry
sat down, and we started talking about that new
game, Super Smasher Sisters. He'd gotten a copy of
it over the weekend, and we decided to make plans to
practice with it after school. Good ol' Larry! He's
always useful for something!

Then Janine sat down. She asked if we'd heard of
this "cool new video game". Total conversation ender.
I didn't want to hear about ponies, princesses or hair-
styling in any stupid girl game. I pretended I was
finished eating and left Larry to take the brunt of
Janine's rainbow of lameness.

I had to get to the library to check my favorite game FAQ site for some information. I'm never a newbie. Before I ever touch a game, I thoroughly research it. Experimenting is for newbies and losers.

That evening, I got to Larry's, and we had 25 practice matches. Larry was better than I thought he'd be, considering he went in completely cold while I'd studied the basics of the system. He almost won a round!

Larry was trying to tell me that he'd gotten some hints on how to play earlier, but hints are for newbies. Stick to the facts. Stick to the practice.

Tuesday

Street pizza

Super Smasher Sisters (rented from Blue Box): 10 consecutive wins online. 4 perfect matches. 1 loss.

I woke up really early today from the sound of something being run over on the road outside our house. Kind of odd how I can't really hear the alarm clock going off, but the sound of some guy smacking an old raccoon on the road got me up right away. It was about 4:00 in the morning when he drove away and just left it there, and for some reason, I couldn't close the blinds and go back to bed.

I just stared at that dead raccoon...for a long time!

The next thing I knew, I was getting out of bed, putting on my slippers, and walking out to the yard and into the street to get that run-over raccoon! I looked around to see if anyone was watching before collecting everything.

Just as quick as my slow feet could move me, I was back in the house with the roadkill. I'm still not sure what I was doing, but wow. It smelled like lasagna! Like warm breadsticks! It smelled like pizza!

Mom was wandering around the house by the time I got to the kitchen with my new raccoon pizza. She stopped and looked at me for a long time. Then she bent over, wrapped her stiff arms around my shoulders, and grunted weirdly.

I think she thought I was giving her a present or something. Weird, weird, WEIRD! So I just gave it to her, and she smiled strangely, like her mouth didn't work so well any more. Then she put it in the oven and charred it real good.

Breakfast was crunchy and real tasty. It was the best pizza I ever had. EVER! Pizza never tasted that delish! I almost forgot to get rid of the bad breath that morning, it was so good.

I have to go out looking for more street pizza later on, because that meal made my day! Now that I think about it, I wasn't really hungry all day after that! At the same time, I'm not so sure that food was the best breakfast for my pro gamer training.

Today at school, we got our new gym uniforms. Gym was officially on the schedule. You probably already know this, but zombies can't run. Zombies can't jump. Zombies can't catch baseballs or kick footballs. Zombies suck at sports!

I discovered that if you ever want to scare or unnerve a zombie, show them a football or a basketball and ask, "Wanna toss the ole pigskin?" or "Wanna shoot some hoops?" These two questions now fill me with disgust and loathing.

Today was track. I'm a zombie, and today was track.

Naturally, gym sucked for me today. The slowest kid
in the whole class, "Death-Butt" Harold, lapped me
while we were doing laps. Well, everyone else was doing
lapS. I was doing "lap".

Just as gym was ending, I noticed Steve hanging out
behind the bleachers with this high school guy. They
had the same kind of hair and the same kind of little
face inside the same kind of big, fat head. They were
brothers—they had to be. Here's the bad part: I knew
that high school guy!

He was one of the guys I'd sharked out of ten bucks

on Saturday! He was the guy who saw me wasting fools at the Game-Stuff during the *Call of Fragenator* tournament! And here's the worst part: Steve's big brother looked right at me! I could just see the recognition in his beady little eyes, as if to say, "So here you are, you little scammin' runt!"

I tried to keep from making eye contact, but I knew I was made. I was a marked man! The last I saw of them, Steve was scowling at me and nodding slowly, as if to say, "Yeah, big brother, I'll get him for you!" I. Hate. Gym!

Coming in from gym class, I noticed a wonderful feature of my body's new anatomy: zombie perspiration! I was only a little bit sweaty, but ewwwww.

My armpits were turning the shirt a little green, and slowly, ever so slowly, I became aware of an odor drifting out into the air. It was like the stink from a sweaty, tired, bottomless swamp's underarm, if a swamp had armpits. I sniffed myself to be sure, hoping it was Harold or some other kid, but nope, it was me. I was going to have to shower. I was going to have to be the FIRST KID to get in the shower!

Ewwww...

Nobody wants to be the first kid in the shower after middle school gym class, but now I HAD to be. I had to wash off the stink before anyone choked to death from it. I turned up the water as hot as I could to make steam. Since I really can't feel hot water now, it didn't bother me, but everyone else backed off!

It was so hot, no one could reach the knobs without getting scalded! Meanwhile, I could just take my time and use my secret weapon against stinkiness: a zip-baggie packet of baking soda. Soap seems to do nothing at all, but baking soda works wonders for some reason. I read it's an "exfoliant", so really helps to remove spoiled, wasted skin and leave normal skin alone. Whatever it does, I can just use a little, and any smells fade away.

Someone called the coach to come turn down the heat in the shower. Even the coach didn't wanna come near the hot water. He saw me in there and said, "Get outta there before you burn yourself!"

I just told him, "Water feels okay to me." The temptation to make myself sound like a tough guy was there, but I didn't need the attention.

I was done pretty quickly and turned the water off so the other kids could shower. .... Okay, I'll admit, I did give in to the temptation a little. As I was going out, I said, "That water's too wimpy, anyway. I usually like it much hotter." The coach didn't even know how to respond to that!

I'll have to look up what kind of zombie I am tomorrow. I sort of have a pulse (it's really weak), so I'm not dead, but no way I'm still human. Nobody can eat what I eat and not get sick. Normal people don't eat rotted guts from roadkill and have them taste like Alfredo noodles. That virus definitely changed me into a zombie...but what KIND?

After school let out, I rented Super Smasher Sisters from a Blue Box DVD terminal outside of the King Burger about a block away from the bus stop. After a few orientation rounds offline, I decided to see how many perfects I could get against the newbies online. Everything was going as expected until I ran into "SanReaper". That guy is too good!

He guessed at my surprise attack tactics right away and developed a counter-strategy! While he couldn't out-react me, he found a way around it: He collected items and power-ups that appeared around the stage. Those bonuses damped or nullified my surprise attack's effectiveness!

I won our first two matches, but they were narrow victories. Then I lost the third match! A close one again, but it seems like he'd figured me out! "SanReaper" is officially a problem. I kind of like challenges, but I don't like problems. I'll need to stay sharper than ever to stop that guy if I ever meet him in a tournament—if he plays tournaments at all!

One thing that annoyed me, though, was "SanReaper's" fighter. He chose "Kittychu"! The weakest, lamest, stupidest character in the line-up! If he chose "Cap'n Punch" or "Star Dog" or "Chain", he'd be much faster and much harder to deal with. Well, not for me, actually. Our matches totally boiled down to mind-games and not the fighters' abilities. If "SanReaper"

choose a high-tier fighter to master, though, he'd be an online phenomenon!

I sent him a comment. He's one of the few players I've ever sent comments to, by the way. "Good game. But why the low-tier character? Why Kittychu?"

He responded, "Because I like Kittychu! LOL!" A newbie answer! You don't master a character because you "like" him! You master a character because he suits your play style!

JEEZ

So maybe I gave "SanReaper" too much credit. Maybe I was just a little sluggish today. Maybe it was that yummy street pizza I had for breakfast!

Wednesday

Stale, moldy Frosted Sugar Tufts and crusty, flaky, sour milk

Super Smasher Sisters: 3 consecutive wins, 4 perfects, 9 losses

Today, I was going to try to stay the sharpest I could possibly get for online pro gamer practice. I noticed Mom had gone shopping recently...and not to the grocery store. Mom had this faint, dumpster-like smell about her. The fridge contained the rest of the evidence.

YOU *DON'T* WANT TO KNOW...

I'm not even going to try to describe what she put in there. It was all gross, but it smelled delicious! In the cupboard, there were some old cereal boxes that must have been thrown away from some outlet store. Mom had gone dumpster-diving for me. Messed up and weird, but I kinda appreciated it.

While I ate, Mom did some dishes. Well, actually Mom did A dish. She was just putting it in the cabinet by the time I finished and headed for the bathroom to make sure everything didn't stink. I also took a little baking powder in a teaspoon. I was hoping it would keep me from killing the class with another accidental death-fart. So far, it's working.

Another period of gym class began today. This time it was dodgeball. HA! Finally, a sport I was good at! No one could touch me.

I could bean anyone I wanted. I didn't have to run or hustle! I just let my reflexes go to work. It was great! The funny thing is, I never liked dodgeball before. Too bad its league is almost nonexistent. Wait, IS there a dodgeball league?

I didn't really sweat in gym today, so I wasn't stinky, and took my sweet time getting ready for lunch. I was the last one in the locker room, and that's when Steve showed up. He just walked right up to me while I was getting my pants on and pushed me down!

Then he kicked me! It must have been a real hard kick, because it sounded like a big stick hitting a tree! It didn't even hurt, though. If anything, Steve looked like he'd hurt his toe from kicking my side. Without missing a beat, he pointed a fat finger in my face and growled, "You got until tomorrow afternoon to get me my brother's money, Bill! Twenty dollars!"

I was confused. "What? I only took ten—" Yeah, I goofed. I REALLY should have just denied everything!

Steve went to kick me again for smarting back, this time in the face. BAM! Another hard kick that didn't hurt. Once more, Steve winced. He shrugged it off but let a curse out as he hopped back a little.

He pointed again. "I said TOMORROW! The ten you took and the ten you owe him! Twenty!" I wish him luck. I'm not giving him Jack if he can't even kick me hard enough to hurt!

THUMP

I remained still until Steve hobbled out of the locker room, then I went to the mirror to make sure nothing was broken. Just a little hair out of place and a slightly purple bruise on my side. The bruise went away before I could pull my shirt back down.

At lunch, I saw Steve hopping a little from his stubbed toe. I almost giggled, but I pretended not to notice. It was another opportunity to practice my poker face!

When I sat down to pretend to eat, Larry told me the Game-Stuff shop was having another tournament this weekend. A Super Smasher Sisters bash! The grand prize was five hundred big ones and a special tournament edition Super Smasher Sisters game pack! Sweet! That was the best news I'd had all week!

Then, as if she knew I was in a good mood today, Janine parked her butt right at our table. "You guys hear the news about Super Smasher Sisters?"

Then it dawned on me. Oh, of course! It's got some great top-tier characters in it, but it's got loads of cutesy characters too. They designed the game to have a super-broad appeal. Of COURSE Janine would like that game too. She's probably into the party game mode, or the board game or "dress up" mode.

Larry asked, "You mean about the tournament?"

Janine squealed, "Noooo, I mean about the downloadable outfits for Wigglystuff, Mr. Flopsy and KittyCHUUUU!" Good grief. That was enough for me. I got outta there before the "Kittychu's so kyuuute!" barrage was unleashed. I wish Janine could take a hint!

The rest of the day was pretty much downhill after that. Steve tried to trip me in the hall, but ha ha!

You can't surprise a zombie. It's like this: If you're coming around a corner and a zombie is coming around that same corner, the zombie's gonna win!

It's like everything moves in slow motion for a little bit of time, then it's back to normal. Like Steve's foot, or those newbies who try to get in the first move. For that split second, I win. Except that split second didn't help during today's practice matches.

It was "SanReaper" again. We were both in a "free-for-all" online arena, and we managed to knock off all the other newbies on the stage. It was just me and him for the "First to ten" contest. The first one to reach ten victories would win! The opening matches all went according to plan. I used my surprise-attack, zombie-style strategy to ambush all of his mistakes. I won the first three matches just like that! I even got two perfect victories.

Then "SanReaper" adapted. He found the clone power-ups! He found every clone power-up in the whole stage! At first, I thought that was silly. If there are ten clones of you on the stage, you can only score a tenth of your damage, and the clones get in your way too! Plus the clones don't do anything but pop when you touch them!

"SanReaper" wasn't after ten clones. He was just setting up one. He made it so he and one clone would approach me at exactly the same time from two different angles. Son of a gun! He made me guess which was him and which was the clone!

After that, I started losing fifty percent of the matches! I need to find a new strategy. Zombie reactions aren't going to be enough in this game! The connection speed was pretty crisp, though. That means "SanReaper" is local. If he turns up at the tournament this Saturday, there's a good chance that I'll lose!

I won, ten games to nine, but it was a toss-up. "SanReaper" could have beaten me if I hadn't guessed right three times in a row. But that's not what upset me. What really got to me is the cutesy little "Yay! I win! Meowchu! Meowchu!" dance he made Kittychu do every time he won a match!

That, and the pink-and-white flower print dress he made Kittychu wear! That flower dress annoyed me for some reason. That's probably why he got the downloadable outfit pack, though—to psych opponents out a little.

It kind of works, I gotta say. At least I know now that it wasn't breakfast slowing me down.

<u>Thursday</u>
Stale, moldy Frosted Sugar Tufts and crusty, flaky,
slightly yellowish sour milk.
Forced to skip practice.

I didn't really need to eat breakfast today. Just
sorta poked at it and tasted a little bit. I was still
full from the "pizza" I ate on Tuesday, and that
kind of bugged me. Sour Sugar Tufts are nice, but
I couldn't stop thinking about how great everything
tasted Tuesday morning, and I couldn't exactly put my
finger on what was the best part.

Before the school bus came, I noticed Mrs. Jefferson
walking her poodle just down the street. She decided
to jaywalk across the road and didn't see the moving
van heading straight for her pink, yappy little dog,
Froufrou. I can't believe that I was actually mentally
cheering for the van to score a hit!

I was going, "Come onnnnn, MOVING VAN!" in my head,
over and over! It disturbs me how disappointed I felt
when Froufrou dodged out of the way just in the nick

of time too. I turned away from the sight of Mrs. Jefferson kissing her poodle on the mouth and going on and on about how relieved she was.

I'd read about the term "crestfallen" before, but I guess I know what it really means now. But that's okay. Mrs. Jefferson's kind of careless about stuff like looking both ways before crossing. Her poodle's luck will run out one day. It's just a matter of time, Froufrou!

Wait. Wow. I can't believe I'm thinking like this. I can't believe I'm hoping for a road kill breakfast tomorrow!

I put baking soda on everything now. I can't really taste it, so it doesn't ruin any flavors for me. It keeps the zombie gas to a minimum, too. I think I'm getting the hang of this new hygiene.

By the time lunch period came, I was feeling pretty relaxed. Except then my whole day was completely ruined by a double ambush from both of my bullies!

I was pretending to eat, sitting with Larry at our usual lunch table spot, when out of the blue, Larry blurts out, "I think Janine likes you, dude!"

I was confused. "What?"

"Not 'like' like. 'Hang out' like."

"WHAT!?"

Then I spotted Janine approaching the table, grinning. On her tray, she had a little plastic, rainbow-colored bag. She put the bag on my tray and said, "I got this present for you!"

In the bag was a "Warturtle", a little plastic figurine of one of the lame, cutesy characters from *Super Smasher Sisters*. I asked, "What the heck is this?"

Janine sat down and said "Give that character a spin. His Snapping Turtleneck stretching attack will let you snipe from a really long way away. And he's got high defense for when you want to hold down the block button. Kittychu's me. But Warturtle's allll YOU! You should play as you!"

She was talking about *Super Smasher Sisters!* I've dedicated most of my life, seven whole YEARS to becoming a pro gamer! I'm not even letting being a zombie stop my dreams! But Janine was giving ME advice on how to game!?!

Then the real ambush came. Larry set me up and Janine knocked me down. Larry said he told Janine what my online game tag was, and Janine came looking for me as "SanReaper." I almost shouted!

Janine's "SanReaper"! Son of a gun!!!

Super cool
SanReaper

=

Kitty
weirdo????

What
the
heck!!??!

I should have guessed from the beginning. Sanrita sells all that cutesy Hiya Kitty merchandise. I should have recognized Janine from SanReaper's sad attachment to cutesy characters with no strategic advantages at all. I should have realized it was Janine from SanReaper's lack of skill and dependency on gimmicks.

I gave "SanReaper" way too much credit! If I'd treated her like the newbie she was, I bet I would have totally owned her all through every last match!

I didn't know what to say! To top it all off, she announced that she was going to compete for the grand prize at the Game-Stuff tournament this Saturday! I was so stunned, I couldn't think. So naturally, I didn't see ambush number two coming.

Steve pulled my chair—hard! He pulled it right out from under me, and I fell on the floor! Then he dumped my food on me. He was shouting, "Where's the money?" while he poured my chocolate milk on me.

He tried to kick my face with his heel, but the surprise was over, and I was ready for what he was going to do. What I WASN'T ready for was what I was going to do! When his foot got near my face, I could see it as

though everything was moving in slow motion. I don't
know what came over me in that split second, though.
My mouth had a mind of its own, and I caught his heel
with my hands and bit him under his ankle!

I bit right through his tennis shoe leather. I bit
through his sock, and I felt a tooth poke a little bit
into his skin.

He tasted like candy! I swear he did! He tasted like a
Strawberry Gushbomb! People taste like candy!

I let him pull his foot back when he yelled. I wanted
to bite down and just rip until I had a nice bit of

Steve to chew, but I didn't. I guess I'm not okay with eating people after all...even when they taste like candy, and they're jerks like Steve who deserve to get their foot bitten off anyway. So maybe I'm not really a zombie. Well, not a people-eating zombie, anyway. Not yet, at least.... Still, Steve tasted good. Too good! If I had it to do over, I would have taken a bigger chomp!

I was sent to the Principal's office for that. I'm the one who almost got his face kicked in, and I got in trouble for protecting myself.

I complained, "So next time, when a bully tries to kick my face, I should just let him break my nose?"

It doesn't matter who starts fights in school, all the teachers and grown-ups care about is who gets hurt afterward. That's why bullies can do whatever they want. As long as they don't leave any scars, they can torture victims and get away with it. I was sent home with a note, thinking, "What do I care? Mom's not going to give a fig anyway. She's a zombie!" Boy, was I wrong.

> Dear Mrs. Stokes:
>
> Your son bit another student's foot in self-defense! We're more worried about getting sued than seeing any justice done. Please punish Bill for *NO REASON!*
>
> Sincerely,
> Principal Buttmunch
>
> Parent's signature
> ✗ _____

I got home and showed Mom the note. She took her time reading it, and I went to my console to practice. The next thing I knew, my power was turned off and Mom was waving the note in my face and grunting at me! I was getting chewed out by my zombie mom for coming home with a note from the principal!

Plus, I was being punished on top of that! Mom wouldn't let me turn the breaker switch back on! She was going to stop me from practicing, even with the big tournament coming up this Saturday!

All she could do was growl at me, but she calmed down long enough to write me a note in her zombie-mom handwriting. It took her a whole hour to write down "No game tonight! Punishment!"

I managed to reason with Mom into getting the power back on so I could do homework, but she guarded my game console all night long!

This was totally unfair! I almost wish I HAD bitten Steve's foot off!

Friday

Skipped Breakfast

Super Smasher Sisters: 20 consecutive wins, 19 perfects

I was still mad when I woke up this morning—not as much as last night, but I needed that training! The food we had Tuesday morning still had me feeling full, though. I got out yesterday's unfinished bowl of Sugar Tufts, but just poked at it, still not in the mood for sour, stinky cereal. Instead, I'm saving it for tomorrow, when I'll need the boost!

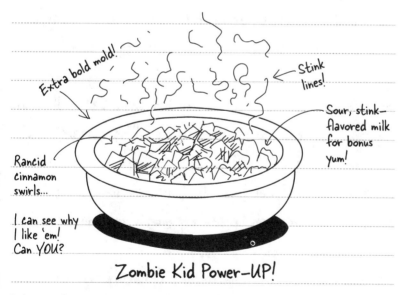

Extra bold mold!

← Stink lines!

Sour, stink-flavored milk for bonus yum!

Rancid cinnamon swirls...

I can see why I like 'em! Can YOU?

Zombie Kid Power-UP!

I turned in the note they sent me home with, and Mr. Philips, our homeroom teacher, accused me of faking

Note from Principal

Dear Parental Unit:

Blah, blah, blah
Yackety smackety!

Parent Signature
Barbara Stokes

the signature. He said it looked like a third-grader signed it. I looked at him and said, "Say that to my mom, and you might get your face chewed off, Mr. Philips!" I didn't need my poker face that time!

Mr. Philips thought I was giving him some backtalk. So, I got a free trip to the Principal's office...again! But you know what? Vice Principal Horshack must've been a handwriting analyzer for the police or something. He saved my bacon when he saw my mom's writing.

He told Principal Washington the signature was legit! I wanted to stand in my chair and go, "Ha! In your face!" but I just sat quietly. Poker face practice time.

100

The vice principal did ask me if Mom was sick or had a stroke, though. I said she has trouble writing, but she still gets around. I don't want any social workers investigating. We'd probably get locked up for science.

If anything's going to derail my pro gamer career, discovery of my or Mom's new zombieness would probably do it for good! They didn't ask any more questions after that, so I guess they didn't suspect anything. I gotta be more careful in school from now on, though. No more biting, if I can help it!

I also found out I had a new nickname when I got to school today: "Snapping Turtle". Great. I didn't need any clues to figure out who came up with THAT zinger.

I can't believe Janine still insists she was trying to pay me a compliment! I'm going to get her back for that! I'm GLAD she's in the tournament now. I'm going to destroy her in front of EVERYBODY. I can't wait until tomorrow!

We had gym class again today. Basketball! A trip to the office, a new nickname, and now this. Basketball.

Larry was on my team with some other guys from homeroom. We were against some other kids who didn't know how to play the game too well either. I hate being a newbie.

I managed to steal the ball when one of the kids from the opposing team got near, but that was all I could do the whole game, since they just stayed away from me after that. Just a class of me trying to run and catch the much faster kids, and a lot of our team losing. I hate losing! In basketball, I'm a loser and a newbie. Gym stinks!

Zombies eat two things!
Great-tasting gross stuff...

...and everybody else's dust!

You'd think all that was enough to log my whole day as totally ruined, but nope. The real trouble hadn't even started yet!

I skipped lunch and just went out to the schoolyard while everyone was eating. I got my food tray and pretended to eat a little, then got out of there before the other kids, especially Larry and Janine, finished their food. I wasn't in the mood for either one of them, but they weren't the problem today.

I noticed Steve at the fence on the other side of the schoolyard. His big brother was there too. Skipping high school again! I could just barely hear them from where I was sitting near the bleachers. Steve's big brother was trying to get Steve to go into the cafeteria and "Get my money!" Steve didn't want to do it. He called me "some kind of crazy freak who bites"!

I had come out into the schoolyard to relax, and instead gotten trapped, alone with bully Steve and his big bully brother! All they had to do was turn around and see me sitting there in the shade of the bleachers!

I knew I'd never make it back into the building without being seen, so I stayed perfectly still, the way Mom was motionless when she caught that squirrel. For a second, I thought they might not see me. Steve even looked right at me a couple of times without realizing I was just across the field. But Steve's big brother noticed!

He pulled out something and started coming right at me. He held it up in his hand. It was a roll of quarters! I read on the internet that when you hold a roll of coins in your fist like that, it's almost like brass knuckles! I was scared, and there was no way I could run away with my slow zombie feet. I was trapped!

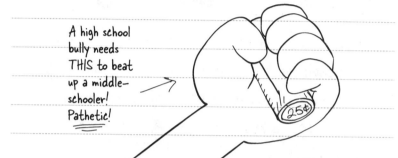

A high school bully needs THIS to beat up a middle-schooler! Pathetic!

Before I knew it, Steve's big brother caught up to me, hit me hard in the pit of my stomach, and pushed me down! Steve just cheered, "Yeah! Get him, Josh!"

Josh growled, "I got him, but you ain't gettin' a dime for this, Steve! If you'd got my money like I told you, I woulda gave you five, but you ain't gettin' nothin'!"

Then Josh yelled at me and punched me in the stomach again! He hit me really hard, and it hurt! Not as much as it should have, but still painful.

I thought he could really mess me up, and there was no way I could escape. Josh hit me again, right in the stomach, and I just curled up and groaned! It was getting harder to breathe, too! And Josh wasn't even getting warmed up!

Josh got to my pocket and stole my money. My prize money! My entrance fee money! All the money I had in my pocket, and I couldn't stop him!

Steve said, "That little freak had all that cash on him!?" Josh laughed and hit me in my stomach! I tried grabbing his arm, but I wasn't strong enough to hold it; it was no use! After a few more hits and kicks in my stomach, Josh started to walk away. I think I started crying. That's what made Josh turn around to gloat!

"How about a knuckle sandwich, crybaby!" he yelled as he leaned in to give me one last punch...in my face. Well, he TRIED to punch my face! NEVER try to punch a zombie's face!!!

I caught his fist before it reached my mouth with both hands, and I clamped down HARD with my teeth! Josh shouted, cried, and kicked at me, but he'd offered me that knuckle sandwich, and I wasn't letting it go until I'd chewed on it a little while!

I wasn't biting through the skin. I'd learned my lesson from Steve, and I wasn't going to leave any scars! I DID crush and chew on his knuckle bones. It was pretty easy, too! I guess zombies have strong jaws for crushing bones. Steve ran after he saw his brother crying. Crying for real! Josh dropped my money, and I let him go.

Needs more spicy mustard!

The last thing I saw was kids and teachers coming out to see what was going on, and Josh and Steve running for it. The brothers got into Josh's car and sped off. I made sure not to wipe the tears from my face. I needed all the evidence I could get to keep the teachers from thinking I somehow beat up two kids who were years older than me! I know, obviously, but with grown-ups, it HAS to be obvious, or YOU'LL wind up getting in trouble too!

I didn't get in trouble and even kept my money, but that whole ordeal stunk! I got out of it because I'm a zombie, but I could've run away if I wasn't!

Larry and Janine kept asking if I was okay, but I wasn't even trying to listen to those two. Janine and I still had to settle things at the tournament tomorrow; I still needed to put her in her place. They weren't going to get me to ease up just because they were pretending to be concerned about me being hurt!

To tell the truth, I did feel a little better after Janine gave me that rainbow band-aid. At least somebody was concerned. Not that it would save her!

Double rainbow, all
the way across
the scar...

What does
it MEAN?

Tonight I turned my phone off, clicked "No chatting"
on my online options, and got right to practice. I
wanted to find "SanReaper" and give her a sneak
preview of the way I was going to totally own her at
the tournament...but she stayed offline! Probably
practicing with Larry. GOOD! If you train with
weaker players, you BECOME a weaker player!

Without "SanReaper" there, I went on an online
rampage! I was unstoppable! I even owned some of
the more famous players that post videos of their
replays online! So I had no doubt in my mind I would've
trashed Janine's character too, if she'd been there.

That's okay. Tomorrow, all my concentration would be
on that tournament. Tomorrow was showdown time,
and it wouldn't be "cute"!

<u>Saturday</u>

Leftover, super-moldy, super-gross Frosted Sugar Tufts. (They were good, too!)

No practice. Super Smasher Sisters tournament happened today.

They'rrRRE GREAT!!

Everything leading up to the tournament went just the way I thought it would. The breakfast I saved from yesterday was nice and ripe. It looked like someone hurled Sugar Tufts in the toilet, scooped them up and served them with a spoon. It was that gross! If you'd smelled it coming out of the fridge like I did, though, you would have thought you were in Candy-Land and that bowl was filled with sugary cream and fresh cinnamon swirls! I didn't even wait to sit down before I started nommin'! My appetite took over, and I just slammed it down with gusto.

I didn't chew a bite. I Just DOWNED that whole bowl in two gulps! It tasted even better than it smelled! It was like someone made a cereal taste like birthday cake frosting with chocolate ice-cream milk! I didn't chew. I didn't take my time. So, it didn't take long for my stomach to mix up the toxins for me...and my butt! That's where my trouble began!

Rumble...
Rumble...
Growl...

UH-OHHh...

I could hear the chemicals going off in my belly like it was a mad scientist's laboratory about to explode! Then it died down, before starting up again! I had gas...ZOMBIE gas!

When I got to the bathroom for a big, heaping spoonful of baking soda to beat the chemicals in my guts into submission, I found only half a baby-sized teaspoon was left! Not nearly enough!

There was no way I could enter the tournament today! Not like this! If that gas erupted from my butt during the event, I'd probably be arrested for an act of terrorism with a weapon of mass destruction!

Tonight at eleven:
Zombie kid hits
game tournament
with DIRTY
NUKE!

News Alert!!

Toxic Zombie Gas!

Big News Channel

Late-Breaking News on Late-Breaking Wind!

3.pts↑ Dow Jones and Stuff

I did the only thing I could do. I had to get rid of the gas right there and then, in the privacy of my own home. I broke wind and belched for the next thirty minutes! While taking a shower, brushing my teeth, and brushing my hair. Belch, poot, belch, poot, belch, poot, poot, poot!

That seemed like it worked. The room had a green haze, though. I could smell the dense uber-stink too, but it didn't gross me out. I guess it takes a lot to gross me out now. Still, it was getting harder to breathe, so I opened a window. A moth flew by and just dropped as soon as it hit the green haze!

Gag!!
Eww!
UGH!!!

Sorry,
Mother
Nature!

I remember thinking how I might have offended the forces of nature and maybe even killed some bald eagles soaring way high in the clouds, but what else could I do? Only a few more blasts, and I was done!

By the time I changed all my clothes, there wasn't any rumbling at all in my stomach. The air was clear, and my deodorant was back in charge! I was home free, and just in time to ride with Mom to the mall. She was going for her weekly magazine and coffee, and I was getting a free trip to the tournament.

Little did I know, the gas I'd released was just the beginning! I was bringing a ticking time bomb of zombie stink, and it was just waiting to ruin everything right when it was all on the line!

I didn't need to wait for Mom to give me my allowance this time. I still had my winnings from last week's tournament to use as the entry fee. It was a hefty fee, too...fifty-five bucks!

I saw some college kids setting up a video camera and a computer so they could stream live coverage of the whole event over the internet! I also saw a representative from *ArcadeStix Magazine* talking to folks. He was checking to see who the top players were and maybe even offering sponsor deals to up-and-coming pro gamer superstars!

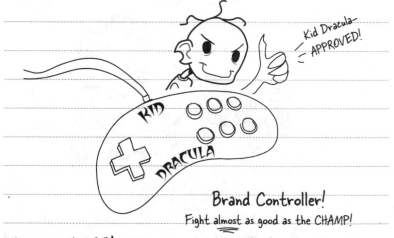

Kid Dracula APPROVED!

KID DRACULA Brand Controller!
Fight almost as good as the CHAMP!

This was HUGE! This was going to kick-start my pro gamer career for sure! I thought that maybe I could even get a sponsor deal if I won big enough!

There were a lot of older kids and some grown-ups entering the tournament. High school guys in one corner were looking my way and making jokes like I didn't belong or was going to get kicked out of the tournament in the first round. The video guys were doing pre-tournament interviews too, but no one wanted to interview me! I was starting to feel out of my league. I was starting to get scared!

Then I saw Larry and Janine. I gotta admit, by then, I was relieved to see somebody, ANYBODY my age in the event! I even forgot my plans to utterly destroy them during the tournament. There were bigger, older, more uppity fish to fry!

We took the whole thing in and stuck together the entire time. I think they could feel the vibe too. Everyone was just ready to write us off as losers because we were small! It was us middle-schoolers against the rest of the world right there. We formed an alliance, like a racing team or something.

Hands
in!!!

Let's kick grown-up butt!

We just gabbed for a while, and get this! Janine has a diary that she keeps records in too! She even has a score-keeping section! It was almost like those days when Larry and I and everybody back at the old cul-de-sac would hang out and talk about games. Janine goes for the cutesy games a little too much, but she's a gamer. Not a pro gamer like me, though.

It has to be more than just for fun to be in my league. Like Larry, it might be okay to let her hang out to keep the bar from getting too low. As long as she keeps that "Hiya Kitty" stuff to herself, that is!

Finally, the tournament started. At first, I thought I was going to have to explain to Larry and Janine that we had to put on game faces for the tournament and that friendship could still be around after a serious competition. Then JANINE, of all people, said, "Look, you guys, I've played in a lot of Squeekimon card game tournaments. We have to get frosty now! No joke!"

I finally caught on to her. Janine's been doing those baby cutesy Squeekimon card game tournaments and wants to step up to the big leagues! That's why she wanted to hang around Larry and me! That's why she kept trying to ride our coattails! Fans and wannabes know a pro when they see one. I can respect that. If she ever worked up the nerve to ask for my autograph, I'd only charge her half price. Perks from being on my side from the beginning.

Oh! Sign my book, "Kid Dracula"!

For you, Janine? Only fifty bucks!

AWESOME!

The tournament was awesome for a while. No one was even close to Janine's level. Heck, no one was even close to LARRY'S level! You should have heard those college video-filming guys laughing at us middle-schoolers beating the tar out of all these older gamers!

They started calling us "The Three Tricycles of the Apocalypse: Kid Dracula, SanReaper and DarthLarry!" And man, were those older kids mad! "Salty" mad! "Salty with tears" mad! Pretty soon, we all had cheering sections! It was hype! "Mad hype!" (I learned those terms from one of the college guys commenting on my match performance.)

This is why I wanted to be a pro gamer. The crowd was into it every time I pulled off a cool move! I felt like a rock star!

I lost my composure and started cheering for Janine during a tough match she had with a real pro gamer who came in from out of town.

Well, I mostly cheered because if she couldn't beat him, it would have been a loss for the little middle school alliance we developed during the tournament.

Kick his BUTT, Janine!

That, and the pro gamer had the nerve to rip off my zombie ambush technique! He must have seen a video replay of one of my matches online! But he was using the wrong character for the strategy.

He was using "Sonatifa"! She's a fast, top-tier character, but he probably picked her because you can see her undies when she kicks high. Ha! I'm glad Janine showed him the door to the loser's bracket!

Everything was going awesome...until the time bomb in my stomach ticked "zero". Right when the winner's finals were going. It was me versus Janine. Larry, who had just defeated that pro gamer guy in the loser's bracket, was waiting for one of us to lose for the deciding match in the loser's finals. The winner of that match would face the undefeated winner, which was supposed to be me, in the grand finals!

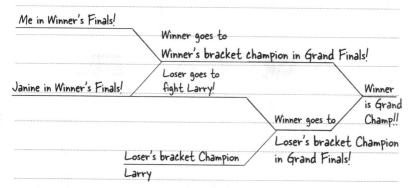

Me in Winner's Finals!

Winner goes to
Winner's bracket champion in Grand Finals!

Loser goes to
fight Larry!

Janine in Winner's Finals!

Winner
is Grand
Champ!!

Winner goes to

Loser's bracket Champion
in Grand Finals!

Loser's bracket Champion

Larry

Unfortunately, I could feel that gas welling up again, and fast! I knew I wouldn't be able to hold it, and the incoming fart was going to hit everyone in that confined room like an atomic bomb! Just from the way it rumbled in my stomach, I knew it was MAJOR!

Janine was winning. I couldn't focus on keeping her from pulling all her little tricks with Kittychu!

I couldn't counter her power-ups, or keep her from starting her little clone-guessing game tricks. I was losing badly every round. At that point, I panicked. This was the end of my career! I knew I'd be known forever as "Kid Choke"!

Janine was wiping the floor with me. She didn't even have to look at the screen anymore! She was staring at me the whole time during her last sixteen-hit combo!

She looked at me and asked, "What's wrong!? Why don't you play right?!" And that really ticked me off. For a while, I got a really evil idea.

I thought that if I let off just a little bitty fart in her direction, I could distract Janine long enough to get the win. She might even pass out, and I would win by forfeit!

Except that'd be cheating. If there's one thing I absolutely can't stand, it's cheaters and bullies, and doing that would have made me both!

So...

I lost.

I threw the match as quickly as I could and got out of there. By the time I got back from the bathroom, everybody was congratulating Larry for winning the tournament! Larry!?! I checked the replays and, wow! Larry took it to Janine in the grand finals! USING WARTURTLE!

Warturtle can attack in two directions at once. He's got every tool you could ever want to use to compete against a player using Kittychu! The matches were really close, but there were a lot of good moves. Wow!

Maybe I could learn a thing or two from Larry. Larry AND Janine!

3rd Place
Kid Dracula

I was mad I lost, but I shook Larry's hand and took home my third place trophy. Janine got it in her head that I threw our winner's finals match, and is saying, "You didn't need to do that to be my friend!"

I swore, "I DIDN'T!" She's not gonna believe until I beat her at the next tournament. So be it!

But I DIDN'T throw the match!!!!!!!!

Suuuure, you didn't!

But I would have beaten you anyway!

We're gonna play some matches on Sunday and get ready for the next tournament. After everyone's seen this tournament online, lots of folks will start using Kittychu and Warturtle. Everyone's seen their potential now! We have to come up with something new!

Tomorrow begins the first practice session of the "Three Tricycles of the Apocalypse" team. We've got T-shirts. I got an email from ArcadeStix—we all did. They want to "talk sponsorship".

Winning!

I'm going to Larry's the first thing after breakfast... whatever crazy, gross breakfast that may be. First, though, I'm going to make sure I have enough baking soda.

Oh, yeah. Whatever you do, don't go into the mall's second-story bathroom—not for at least a week! Not without a gas mask!